Mr. Fox

Author

Sue Dickson

Illustrated by

Leigh Anderson

Page Layout & Design: Jean Hamilton & Leigh Anderson

Original Character Design: Norma Portadino • Adapted Character Design: Chip Neville & Jean Hamilton

Copyright © 1998 Sue Dickson • International Learning Systems of North America, Inc. • Oldsmar, FL 34677
Printed in the United States of America • ISBN: 6-56704-613-4 (Volume 6)

F G H I J K L M N—CJK—05 04 03 02 01 00

Vocabulary

1. kitten

2. mitten

3. ox

4. past

5. rug

6. truck

7. who
(ho͞o)

Sight Words

8. Mr.

9. Mrs.

10. so

11. we

Mr. Fox and Mrs. Pig . . .

3

met a cat who had a wig.

Mr. Fox and Mrs. Cat . . .

met a dog who had a hat.

Mr. Fox and Mr. Dog . . .

met a duck up on a log.

Mr. Fox and Mrs. Duck . . .

met a pup up in a truck.

Mr. Fox and Mrs. Pup . . .

11

met a bug up in a cup.

Mr. Fox and Mrs. Bug . . .

met a kitten on a rug.

14

Mr. Fox and Mrs. Kitten . . .

15

16   met a hen who had a mitten.

Mr. Fox and Mrs. Hen . . .

met an ox who had a pen.

Mr. Fox and Mr. Ox . . .

19

met a frog who had a box.

Mr. Fox and Mrs. Frog . . .

met a man who had a dog.

Mr. Fox and Mr. Man . . .

23

met a pig who had a pan.

Mr. Fox and Mrs. Pig . . .

met a cat who had a wig.

Mr. Fox and Mrs. Cat . . .

met a dog who had a hat.

Said Mr. Fox, "We met in the past."

"Let's get the pals . . .

and jig so fast !"

31

The End